VOICES IN DIVERSITY

Also by Ko Won

Original Poetry

THE TURN OF ZERO (1974)
SOME OTHER TIME (1990)

Translations

CONTEMPORARY KOREAN POETRY (1970)
SOUTH KOREAN POETS OF RESISTANCE (1980)

Scholarly Work

BUDDHIST ELEMENTS IN INDIA:
A COMPARISON OF TRISTAN TZARA, TAKAHASHI
SHINKICHI, AND THEIR FELLOW POETS (1977)

VOICES IN DIVERSITY

POETS FROM POSTWAR KOREA

Selected and Translated with a Preface by

Ko Won

Cross-Cultural Communications
Merrick, New York
2001

Published with the generous support of the Korean Culture and Arts Foundation.

We are also grateful to the New York State Council on the Arts and the National Endowment for the Arts whose past seed grants, in part, have contributed to making this publication possible.

"Late Arrival" by Ha Chong-o and "Becoming Water" by Kang Ŭn-kyo first appeared in *Luna* (University of Minnesota, 1999). Ackowledgment with thanks is accorded to the editor and publisher.

Published in the United States by
Cross-Cultural Communications
239 Wynsum Avenue, Merrick, NY 11566-4725/USA
Tel: 516-868-5635 Fax: 516-379-1901
E-mails: cccpoetry@aol.com / cccmia@juno.com

Library of Congress Cataloging-in-Publication Data

Voices in diversity : poets from postwar Korea / selected and translated with a preface by Ko Won.— 1st ed.
p. cm.
Includes bibliographical references.
ISBN 0-89304-885-2 (hardcover) — ISBN 0-89304-886-0 (paperback)
1. Korean poetry—20th century—Translations into English.
I. Ko, Won, 1925- .
PL984.E3 V65 2001
895.7'1408—dc21

2001041186

Book design by Bebe Barkan
Printed in the United States of America

To my wife Grace Young-Ah
with love

Preface

This anthology contains 92 poems by 37 poets who were born in or after 1945. The end of World War II, August 15, 1945, is an epoch-making date in the history of contemporary Korea in that it brought about Korea's liberation from Japanese rule. I thought that it would be interesting and meaningful to look at the poetic realm of those who witnessed the new political, social, and cultural developments in postwar Korea. The youngest poet represented in this book was born in 1962.

The number of published poets in South Korea (the Republic of Korea) alone is said to be well over a thousand; most of them belong to the postwar generation. It was certainly not easy for me to select fewer than fifty. The availability of source material and the translatability of the available work also limited the selection of poems. I have excluded the poets residing abroad and those in North Korea; (and three South Korean poets, with regret, because of copyright problems*); it seems reasonable to assume that these two areas may be more suitable for separate books. All the personal names are rendered in Korean fashion with the family name coming first: for example, Chang Chŏng-il instead of Chŏng-il Chang.

Both the translation and publication of this new kind of collection is supported by the Korean Culture and Arts Foundation in Seoul. I am particularly grateful for the foundation's translation grant for this project. I also want to express my profound gratitude to my dear old friend, S. ["Sam"] E. Solberg of the University of Washington who read the manuscript and made a great deal of invaluable suggestions.

My special thanks go to my wife, Young-Ah (Grace), for her mental and emotional support, as well as encouragement throughout the time period that I worked on this book. I am also extremely pleased to work with my fellow poet, Stanley H. Barkan of Cross-Cultural Communications.

—Ko Won

Summer 1999
Northridge, California

*See About the Poets

Table of Contents

ROOMS

If you have two rooms,
you need two chests,
two calendars,
two phones,
two fans,
and two heaters.

If you have two rooms,
a TV set is on in each room,
a radio is on in each room,
a man sings and claps his hands,
and the other cries and kicks the floor.

If there are two rooms,
loneliness doubles,
sadness doubles,
the flow of tears doubles,
worry doubles,
and concern doubles.

Nevertheless,
wisdom doesn't double,
peace doesn't,
joy doesn't,
pleasure doesn't double,
nor does laughter.

If there are two rooms,
the father and his son
each locks his room tight.
They don't see each other for a long time,
nor do they talk to each other for a long time;

each lies on his bed,
either smokes
or finishes smoking.

With two rooms,
three rooms,
four rooms,
....
there will be more walls
and more walls.

THE "CENTRAL" AND ME

He is close to the "Central."
He always tells me:
I'm going to report it to the "Central";
the "Central" is watching that;
the "Central" has prohibited it;
the "Central" doesn't like it;
that is different from the "Central" line.

Where is the "Central"?
What and who is the "Central"?
What is this guy who claims that he was appointed
by the "Central" which is neither visible nor audible?
His repeated reference to the "Central"
makes me feel uneasy about the "Central."

The "Central" is located very far from us,
says he,
and the others come from an extremely high place
which we cannot reach.
When this mission is accomplished well,
he will be going to the "Central,"
he dreams.

But the "Central" doesn't call him
after ten years of service;
the "Central" won't send him a notice.
Why doesn't the "Central" call him up?
Why doesn't the "Central" remember him?

BLACK BOOK COVER

That book!
A mysterious book
with a black cover design.
A book whose cover is too heavy,
a book one hand cannot open.
That book!

That book which could be open,
it seems to claim
with the whole body alone,
the entire spine.
Oh my gosh,
that, that, that thing.

A book! A book! The book!
The thing covered with black lacquer,
a black book,
a black casket,
a mysterious cover design.

MAYBE

(A classroom in a tent.
It's raining on rice bags.)

We made a jeep
with rubber shoes.
A U.S. army came over,
and you got off.

American soldiers were chattering
and left after saying maybe.
So you were named maybe.
You, a maybe chewing American gum,
a maybe getting whipped on the calf.

A maybe throwing tangerines at the blackboard.
The kids gathered to pick up broken pieces, and you
stood behind with hands on waist;
a maybe like an American soldier.

A maybe stronger than a girl of mighty sinews;
a maybe who gives a mighty girl a kick.

That maybe left one day, unnoticed,
with American soldiers;
it's raining here now.

A maybe who didn't even know his name;
we get no news from abroad.
Grown up, everybody is like an orphan, anyway.
A maybe whom we won't call maybe anymore.

VENDING MACHINE

I wanted orange juice,
but I pushed the button for coffee.
It's a horrible habit.

A horrible habit drags me along.
A hypnotic habit drags me
around like a sleepwalker
in a foggy land of habit.

I must collect my mind, clearing up
the dense fog that wrapped
fixed ideas in my brain. Attention!
Now I'm drinking unexpected coffee.

There is an eye that works with a vending machine
that turns the light on for a coin;
let's call it a whore,
or call it a golden church.
Who is the pimp who collects money
from the vending machine?

If you know the power of money,
just put it in,
and the whore of a vending machine
will give you a cup of saccharin-like pleasure.
If the machine carried a cross,
would it give you God's orange juice?

THE SOUND OF DRYING GLUE

2 a.m., there comes
from behind the wall
the sound of drying glue,
now not starchy, which
used to adhere in the tiny space
between the wall and paper
in the dry autumn air.

Empty, 2 a.m.;
the space between the wall
and wallpaper expanding,
the darkness behind the wallpaper
makes a sound, like invisible life.

Loud are the fall insects.
While the retired summer is drying
the rain-wet wallpaper,
I in the garden
tread on grassblades, one by one.
There drip the cold drops of water
to the ground—toward winter.

TREMBLING OF DUST

The down
stuck to a tiny spot
is moving.
The mind smaller than the spot
shakes deep down like the splitting earth.

The anger which couldn't be vented up to the end
has been banded together in a very small body
and is now sinking to the bottom of a continent.
Yet the roaring uprise
remains alive.

Wet with sweat, tottering and bent,
the dust at the end of the down
trembles slenderly.
Our lives are hung on the indicator
of a seismograph.

SPRING WIND

The palm of immense tenderness.
Where is this coming from?
The buds waiting to come out
on the branches where the sap rises
open their little breasts in the warm,
shiny wind filled with water.

CHANGHWA AND HONGNYON

Out of the flowers that fill my eyes,
I pick Changhwa and Hongnyon to read,
the rose and red lotus flower in the tale.

The mist rolled out of the broken branches of streetside trees as Changhwa walked down an endless road. The moment she opened the door, holding clothes for the unborn child she had brought along the way, she collapsed. Hongnyon ran hard. She rushed into a stranger's house. After waiting, Changsoe drew a knife. It was foggy all around. Thick and sick. Her skirt was flying in the wind.

Roses in a church garbage cart
and lotus blossoms in a pond
are getting rotten.
So are my eyes.

Changhwa and Hongnyon—female characters in the *Tale of Changhwa and Hongnyon*, an anonymous novel of the Yi Dynasty dealing with a family tragedy caused by a stepmother.

AN ACCOUNT OF THE UNFORGETTABLE

My country used to be a colony.
Born in a land controlled by strangers, now living
in a land taken care of by old war-buddies,
I am not master of my own house.
All I have are some rags passed down to me
and my life;
there is no comfort in sleep.
I am aware of the formalin odor in our sleep,
my sleepless friend's death,
and a dream in death; a pushpin
is stuck into the dream.

Yes, our country taught us how to be slaves,
slaves of a dream.
I know this extraordinary myth:
flesh betrayed by bones,
bones betrayed by flesh,
a foreign dream
between flesh and bones,
and the dream war.
We are confined
between myth and reality,
a formalin-smelling dream.

My friend was shot to death in April.
I remember his voice reading from a book
when we were in grade school.
It's been more than ten years since he died,
yet I still smell formalin when I open a book.
When I have my students read aloud.
I hear his voice;
he is free after death.

No face here,
nor eyes, nose, mouth, or ears;
only the voice.
I am only reminded of the voice,
saying, Oh God!

I hear the grumblings of a poet
who was arrested last night;
he is said to have denied the charge
more than three times.
What a pre-noun of our fatherland,
a pre-noun prefixed to one's name.
Dropping his head, he said:
"The poet's casket is heavy, and I forgot
all the beautiful words and songs."
Dreadful is the night he doesn't return;
frightful is the land where he cannot return;
fearful am I living in the land he doesn't return to.
But I never, never forget anything.
Oh, my country, let me remember
the name, our name we call,
freedom.

AT ENTRANCE TO THE DARK SUBWAY

Evening. Listen, a flock of pigeons
fluttering their feathers in applause.
This the plaza where we shouted hurrah
flapping torn cotton cloths,
our arms bleeding.
History always comes to my mind
while walking.
As the sun sets behind the central government buildings,
I hear, under the gloomy walls of the old palace
shadowed by the Japanese government-general,
some passwords exchanged on a walkie-talkie,
army songs, whistles, and heavy sounds of the heels.
Strangely, today I hear
the words of a friend who said no drink made him drunk
and his guffaw, pointing at a news company.
Blood might be rising in his arms or heart
besides the breaking sound of a fountain.
Listening to the applause of pigeons
fluttering in the evening,
I remain standing at the dim entrance to the subway
and watch the endless disappearances of people for somewhere.
A few cars are parked in front of the hotel across the street,
and a starving man falls down to the ground.
Azaleas in a flower garden look redder.

WASHING A SHOVEL IN A DARK RIVER

What flows is not just a river, is it?
We are the same;
we go out to a riverside, wash a shovel,
and throw away the sorrow we dig up.
Watching the river deepen itself naturally,
I squat down, smoke cigarettes,
and go back; that's all.
One life entrusted to a shovel shaft
gets dark and dark like this;
the moon rises above the water
rotten at the bottom of a tributary river.
We are the same;
washing a shovel in the flowing water
as it gets dark, we have to go back
to a village of hungry people.

NIGHT TRIP

At night
everything gets lower
and gets crooked.
Though I walk straight,
the road staggers.
Though I stand straight,
the road goes down.
I can't go on with eyes open
on the road I could travel with eyes closed.
With my clothes on, I can't stand
on the land where I could stand naked.
It's strange, at night
it's nothing but total darkness
which cannot light up even one eye.

SMOKE

Only after the night passes, can I go to you.
Where I walk around, there are only trees
that have dropped their leaves.
My heart gets hot while nothing really exists near me.
My somebody,
I can't go ahead lightening the road myself.
After a few drops of clean water falls down,
warm drops from somewhere in a human being
such as tears, blood, or bones, getting cold,
the light of a metaphor will still be alive tomorrow.
My somebody, therefore,
why don't you come the dark way and hug me?
Trees, ignoring me, keep dropping leaves,
and the dark mountain catches them to cover my heart.
The fallen leaves burn in my heart,
and I, becoming smoke, ascend to the sky.
You will be glad to see me there.

LATE ARRIVAL

A bird came down
from the sky when it was sleeting.
The silt that had pushed the sea far away,
now coming up above the horizon, caught the sky.

The low tide, reluctant to withdraw at its set time,
had drawn me close, then pushed me away.
When I stood straight after tottering back and forth,
crabs stopped crawling.

Because I arrived late, I had no idea
as to whether the bird came to see me
or I came to wait for the bird.
I just came vacuously to a vast place,
for there was something I longed for.

I wanted to go into the village with the sky on my back,
but the silt didn't hand it over to me
and released me to go on the way to land in sleet.
The flat horizon of the world became overcast,
and the cold wind turned me around.

With faltering steps, I muttered: where,
where did the bird go?

MT. MUDŬNG

A
mou-
tain of de-
spair with a head
shaven, a whole naked
body of anger, love, silence,
of a great war whoop, witness,
death, resurrection, eternal life, living,
sacrifice, hard breath, surge, an ardent wish,
dreaming, dreams, yet a mountain of reality, of
blood, fully bloodstained, a religious mountain and, ah
so, so explosive, difficult, strong, rising, with an open eye,
opening eyes, a mountain of the dawn, hope, and of equality—
all, all composing the summit, an equal mountain, of the earth; it's
our mother who shields us, protects us intensely, amply: oh, our mother.

Mt. Mudŭng—located in the vicinity of Kwangju, a southwest city, and it is generally regarded as a spiritual symbol of the local people.

A BIRD LEAVING HOME

A bird
never leaves its trace.
On the branch where it sat,
its weight only shakes for a while;
a bird
leaves no reflection.
In the air once it has flown away,
there is no sign of its body's passage.
Is it because it has no past?
No bird has
its odor either.
It cries with no tears.
Only with a totally emptied body,
it can fly against the storm.
With dreamy, desiring eyes,
a bird stares at tomorrow's bush
and into the gusty wind.

FROM A WINTER-TREE TO A SPRING-TREE

A tree is a tree
by its own body.
All, with its entire body, a tree becomes a tree.
Its entire body unclothed at 19 degrees
below zero, 20 degrees below zero. It's rooted
with its head raised on the ground,
standing naked, defenseless,
standing for punishment with two arms up,
straight up punished, incurring punishment.
But no, oh no, it can't be like this.
Anxious, full of soul, burning inside, inward,
resisting, refusing, from below zero to above
zero 5 degrees, 13 degrees above the ground,
up it goes, pushing hard, pushing up.
For a breakthrough, breaking itself,
the whole body crumbling, bursting, the tree
sticks out buds with its own tongue, and they
slowly, gradually, suddenly, turn to green leaves;
striking the April sky, blowing the blue,
a tree becomes a tree with its entire body.
Ah, at last, to the last, after all,
a flowering tree is a flowering
tree with its own body.

BECOMING WATER

If we become water and meet,
wouldn't we be glad of any dry place?
If we, standing along tall trees, flow like
the booming sound of rain, wouldn't we be?

Only if we flow and lie down at sunset
in a river that gets deeper by itself,
and if we make the roots of dead trees wet;
if we reach the sea—ah, still
a shy maiden, how glad would we be?

But now we are
meeting as fire.
A bone, already charred, touches
everything inflammable.

My friend, waiting far, far away,
let us meet as flowing water
after that fire is gone.
Talking in the sound of a dying fire,
why don't you come like the sky
clean, wide open, and untrodden?

IN THE FOG

There in the fog are
men and women who are waiting
and who have stopped waiting.

In the fog are
men and women who are waking up
and who have just
started sleeping.

And now those who are then
gradually becoming an island
and who are then gradually
becoming water, dancing water.

Ah, all in the mist.

Men and women
who have not met yet and those
who have already parted are
together planting on the earth
the seeds of their dream
abundant as saliva.

SLEET

It's sleeting.
Unable to be either refreshing rain
or brisk snow,
breaking, whirling, and spinning
in the empty space,
it sleets traceless.
It's sleeting on the roads I've been running on,
all the minds pacing up and down,
the agonized souls rising up and up again
to find no Heaven.

The fog scatters in the fog.
Darkness scatters in front of the dark.
Here the darkness picks and throws
a drop of blood, a piece of flesh
wandering about in the void;
here a parting sobs out
at another parting.

It's sleeting.
Unable to be either refreshing rain
or brisk snow,
you, the sleet one day,
breaking down the whole dark world,
and then a grass-flower drawing a sigh
for a moment after a moment.

SICKNESS

Since my face began to look like a strange
    landscape painting,
I have been an old tree with branches cut away.
The tree has gotten lost
    like a sentence without a subject.

Sometimes choking darkness
    undigested in the stomach
makes me open my eyes, twisting
    half-a-piece of soul.
There lies a hard body where the red times
that faced cruel death are beautifully folded.

Man, it's beginning to put on autumnal tints.
Ah, man, it's turning yellow.

AN EMPTY HOUSE

I am writing
    as I lost love.

Goodbye to those short nights,
wintry fogs wandering around windows.
Goodbye to the totally ignorant candle lights,
sheets of white paper that were waiting for horror,
and to tears which used to represent hesitation.
Wishes that are no longer mine, so long.
    So long!

Groping for the lock, now I, blind,
    lock the door.
A poor thing, my love
    is locked in an empty house.

RAILROAD

The reason why a railroad is a railroad
is the fact which makes you unable to meet it
is so stubborn right now.
It has been raining all the time,
cooling down the railroad's heat
to enable its cast iron to endure till today.
Instead of tumbling down,
it has endured as a railroad, which means
the hope of the people who walked on it
has been depressing, heavy on their shoulders.
People did not start leaving for somewhere,
for something because a railroad was built.
Separated into two directions,
a railroad to the South Sea
and another to the ceasefire line
have each been divided;
crossing the Han River Bridge,
one goes to Inchon
and the other to Suwon.
In front of my feet still stuck to the platform,
the railroad is insisting, long, and dark,
exactly as hope has always been.
The fact that a railroad is a railroad means
we haven't yet given up the hope for
meeting somewhere in the long, long future.
A road is this long and this far
everywhere, anytime;
it means that earlier leaving
was that much more serious.
Meeting was prepared for before a road.

Getting close to my ankles
as I haven't left yet,
the railroad soon becomes
many welts of a whip in my heart.

YONGSAN STATION

Brave enough to have visited here
in a thick fog, they got lost.
Nobody seems to be interested in the shabby bags
they took with them or the long-forgotten mass songs
they would sing. This is Yongsan Station
where the faceless women get grabbed at random;
the fog grows thicker as time passes
surrounding these brave women.
When the fog brings in a dark night, the city will hide
their thick make-up with its tricky lights.
The fog thickens for their dirty livelihood.
The sounds of the steam whistles leaving scream for nothing,
but it makes the staying heart feel the shock.
The lives wriggling in the waiting room for a Hunam line
and under the Yomch'on Bridge, the lives
only left with tatters flutter, unrooted, in the cold wind.
In the mist of life, that of the natural outcome,
coming and leaving are natural; so is meeting;
and so is selling women's flesh at Yongsan Station.
Ch'ungnami, who said all this, a pimp king of this area,
later in jail, was said to be released in five years.
Has he also left, giving up this market?
Or he, too, feeling sorry for people leaving shabbily,
sometimes longing for those women
at a ticket gate or a bus stop, has decided
to mingle with them and play cards in a room
smaller than a jail.
Is he now striking me this hard, really hard,
for being brave enough to visit this place?

LAND PHYSIOLOGY

Sow seed
in the ground;
it makes a field.

But what if you don't?
There in the ground
guns and swords are piled.

UNTITLED

Why do birds die, flying
way out to an invisible land?
Tree leaves that know their thought
fall down to the ground and cover
the backs of insects
who don't know where to go.

A BEAN

Who dropped this?

It may have slipped out of a hole
in a bundle carried by a worn-out
old woman from the country who was
on the way to her youngest daughter.

A blue bean
tramped down, tumbling
on the asphalt plaza
in front of the station.

I picked up that wonderful life,
got out of the city,
and planted it deep, very deep
in a patch across the river.

At that time, the sunset
was everywhere watching me.

THE NIGHT IN SEOUL

How many mountain ranges do I
have to go over to reach you?
A red ant
is crossing plastic roses
one by one.

How many, so many stairs do I
have to ascend to wake you up?
Riding an elevator that is lit by itself
and throbbing with its whole body,
I am going up inside
your sleeping body at midnight.

How can I suck a light?
A moth
with its tongue set on end
is glaring at streetlights all night.

A DEAD TREE STILL STANDING

The young moon's eyebrows
    winking, blinking
    opening, closing
enjoy caresses.
An invisible cloud's hand may be
touching an invisible moon's body;
while being pushed back slowly,
    pitch-black
    dissolute
the moon dies and comes back to life
    winking, blinking.

Trees in the wood shake, seen dim,
like the moon's toes.
A dead tree leaning over the night's railing
still keeps standing there
and steals are flowing moon's body
    all night long.
watching the blinking eyebrows
through a chink in the door.

A MUMMY

I get old even after I die.
My face burns even after I die.

If a person's life can be likened
to taking a turn round the globe,
I am now at the Sahara.

The sea of menopause has completely dried out,
and clams are turning upward.

At every step I make,
thousands of fingers that used to hold my wrist
break and get trampled on, hot,
under the soles of my feet.

The covering rags tatter, flapping.
It's snowing in black.

THE HEART

What is the dagger after?
What does the point of a sword aim at?
On a broad road in broad daylight,
in a dark alley, why, why
does the dagger set its eye on the heart?
And how is the heart so grand
toward the dagger?

MASSACRE

It was a certain day in May,
a day in May of 1980,
a certain night in May 1980 at Kwangju.

I saw it at midnight; I saw
normal police changing to the combat-police unit.
I saw at midnight the combat police
changing to the military.
At midnight I saw American civilians
getting away from the city.
At midnight I saw all the vehicles
entering the city being held up.

Ah, what a dismal midnight it was!
Ah, what a planned midnight it was!

It was a certain day in May,
a day in May of 1980,
a certain night in May 1980 at Kwangju.

I witnessed at midnight a bunch of soldiers
armed with rifles and swords.
I witnessed at midnight a bunch of soldiers
like barbarian invaders.
At midnight I saw them
like barbarian plunderers.
At midnight I saw them
like devil incarnates.

Ah, what a dreadful midnight it was!
Ah, what an exposed midnight!

It was a certain day in May,
a day in May of 1980,
a certain night in May 1980 at Kwangju.

Midnight,
the city was a red heart thrown into utter confusion.
Midnight,
the streets were bloody rivers flowing like lava.
Midnight,
the wind was blowing the killed girl's bloody hair.
Midnight,
the night was digging out children's eyes,
projecting like bullets.
Midnight,
the slaughterers were moving the mountain of bodies
somewhere.

Ah, what a horrible midnight it was!
Ah, what a night of plotted massacre!

It was a certain day in May,
a day in May of 1980,
a certain night in May 1980 at Kwangju.

Midnight,
the sky was red, a bloody cloth.
Midnight,
the streets were overwhelmed with crying families.
Midnight,
Mt. Mudŭng rolled up its clothes over its face.
Midnight,
the Yŏngsan River stopped breathing.

Ah, the massacre at Guernica
    couldn't have been this gruesome.
Ah, no devil's plot could have been
    as elaborate as this.

THIS FALL

This fall, I am a prisoner in a blue uniform.
Roped and chained,
I am being dragged to somewhere.

Where am I going this time?
A jail in Chonju? Taejon? or Taegu?

The patrol wagon which I am in
runs through a field, passing
the familiar streets, mountains, and rivers.

Oh, I wish I could get off the wagon here.
I wish I could go to the farm where my mother
picks red peppers in the hot sun over there.
Oh, I wish I could get off there,
and I could go to the farm where my father
cuts rice plants with a sharpened sickle.
I wish I could get off here and go to a river bank
where children make goats fight with their horns;
I wish I could work together and play with them.
With my untied waist and unchained limbs,
I wish I could walk wild through the field.
I wish to run the bank around fields with arms wide open.
If I find breathing hard, I would rest and go again;
if thirsty, I would drink well water to quench my thirst;
if hungry while I keep going,
I would pick the up-grown white radish and eat.
When it becomes dark and I become exhausted, I wish
I could go home alongside returning birds.
But the transfer wagon never stops for me.

It passes by and crosses rivers
and turns a mountain foot at dusk.
At a village over there, dinner-cooking smoke comes up.
I, this fall, am a prisoner in a blue uniform.
This blue fall, I am a prisoner in a blue uniform.

A GAME

The sunlight,
a squirrel's tail in size,
is lying on the doorsill
in jail.
I'd like to cut it into slices
with scissors and swallow,
gulping and gulping down.
The frozen body may melt
like the spring snow.

AT MT. CHUWANG

Autumnal sunshine.
When I stand before this austere transparency,
It seems I have to take my hat off.

Tree leaves grown old nicely make sounds, rolling;
those still alive rub against each other for clean sounds.
Nobody goes farther for the way ahead,
and each one, looking back at the way behind,
sticks a cigarette between his haggard lips.

What kind of appearance, standing in the autumn sun,
can make a human being appear to be ripe?

If I am supposed to wait, watching
the premonition of a certain time to come,
like a persimmon left alone, watching on top
which no pole can reach,
in what posture should I sit
within this cleanness?

A LETTER TO MY ELDER BROTHER

Brother, I'm indebted to other people for my living,
and I choose to do only disgusting things,
and yet, you know, I keep talking big and easy.
    Money is not all for life.
    Lead an honest life, and you'll
    survive for sure.
I just say these sorts of things easily, in vain.
And you tell me:
    You fool, you haven't had hard time
    enough to know life.
Our family went broke, but you and I
managed to go to Taejon for study;
we walked to and from school for miles
eating mugwort soup we cooked
and some leftover noodles.
    You talk about our self-boarding
    secondary-school days.
You paid tuition for your only brother first,
and you got suspended from school.
On a day when your teacher who couldn't be
aware of the situation slapped you on the cheek,
long-controlled, bitter tears streamed down your face
out of chagrin, you said.
    You talk about those days of suffering.
    Every time you do, you're choked,
    and I shed tears, saying
    no more, please.
But, Brother, don't say money, money;
you are hungry for money, but I hate it,
I even hate the sound "em."
    I murmur at random.
Then you get up, somewhat embarrassed, and feeling

pity for this shabby-looking brother, you take out,
with a rustle, some hard-earned paper money for me.
    Hey, baby, don't smoke too much.
You spit it out before you go out.
The words of a cheapskate and my beautiful talking
always come to an end like that.
This might be affection between brothers
which people call tedious, even dirty.
Make money or not, whatever; that's nothing.
I am happy about life and secure as long as
I feel deeply the so-called tedious affection of this kind.
You see, that's why I choose to have my own way
and how I insist on going at you with this and that.
Sometimes, because of that kind of fun,
you also add some unreasonable remarks.
Brother, I know that.

THE SŎMJIN RIVER I

Walking along in the dry weather,
look at the Sŏmjin River.
There gather and flow brook-streams
never interrupted no matter how much drawn,
exactly like the veins of Chollado.
When it gets dark, the river brings its banks
white clover flowers like cooked rice
and milkweed flowers like charcoal fire,
so the banks put them on the head.
The river collects darkness around
a riverside village not shown in any map
and grass not entered in a botanical encyclopedia,
killing the darkness by hanging
flower lanterns on sunburned foreheads.
When feeling choked after flowing on and on,
Sŏmjin calls the current going to the Yŏngsan River
and gives a tight hug of affection;
then it turns around the thick waist of Mt. Chiri.
Look at that Sŏmjin, walking along!
Mt. Chiri, washing in the evening river
and rising with guffaw, shouts at Mt. Mudŭng:
    Sŏmjin can't be dried up by a handful of guys
    that dare draw it off, can it?
    That's impossible. Am I right?
Mt. Mudŭng nods its yes.
Look at Mudŭng's shiny head.
Look at Sŏmjin, walking alongside.
A handful of ill-bred sons-of-bitches
never can dry it up.

Sŏmjin River—runs from North Cholla province, through South Cholla and South Kyongsang provinces, to Namhae (The South Sea).
Chollado—name of a province in the south, including North and South Cholla.
Yŏngsan River—runs from South Cholla to Sŏhae (The West Sea).
Mt. Chiri—stands among three provinces: South Kyongsang, North Cholla, and South Cholla. Its range forms the watershed between the Naktong River (in South Kyongsang) and the Sŏmjin River.

THE SŎMJIN RIVER III

You must have become attached to it.
While looking at the sunset,
sparkling ripples, countless, come and fall
deep, deep in you and the riverside over there;
you must have grown, unknowingly
fond of the depth of the water.
As flowerets bloomed and faded again,
also grass seeds faded,
all frosty in white,
you always came close here
inclining to the hoary grass leaves;
when you were coming, the sun set,
and you were thirsty in front of water;
you were sad and happy,
your shoulders trembling with love.
Your yearning must have rooted deep in water.
Returning from the waterside in the evening
to a place with no one waiting,
you became intimate with each
stone and grass on this road;
you must be in love with this land.
With love
that has to grow,
you look from afar at the village
where lights come alive one after another.
You must have already packed
beautiful love
on your haggard back.

BARLEY SEEDS

High up is the moon.
Harvest is just over in our land,
and I walk along a path in the field,
dirt path.
Longing for the soil to place
a grain of barley on it
and the soil to cover a grain of barley—
that's how I've been living.
That's it.

COOKED RICE AND REVOLUTION

Let's suppose every one
of the people in this land,
with no exception,
in the morning and evening
without skipping a single day
captures all, controls all.
And yet suppose nobody
would be greedy or interested
in his/her own power.
Say, rather,
within a full stomach,
within their satisfaction,
like the cooked rice of life that is
forgotten quietly like the air.
Staid is a revolution;
sedate is love.

A MORNING GLOW

As I sharpen a sickle, cleaving the early-morning darkness,
my mind as refreshing as spring water
rises along the opening eastern glow.
As I grind a sickle hard on the tough face of a whetstone
at a fountain-site around the corner of the dew-wet yard,
the blade gets whetted in pure white
while pretty gray powder comes up,
and beads of sweat stand on my hot brow.
I know, with an overflowing joy of strength,
my father and neighbors, lifetime farmers,
must have sharpened a sickle early every morning;
now here, the more I whet it
the blue blade in my heart also gets sharper.
I wish I could cut a lot of things with its edge,
especially, the reasons for the endless deficit farming.
Actually, though, it couldn't ever even cut that morning
"New Village" broadcast from a local government office
which shouts the fancy slogan of Welfare Farm Villages.
Only with great wishes for constant work,
work coming before anything else, I only sharpen
a sickle for grass cutting every morning, and then
there spreads a blood-red glow way out in the eastern sky
and hope trembles at the end of the sickle at last.

TREADING ON BARLEY

On this sunny good day,
filled with the fresh spring sentiment,
warm-hearted, we keep treading all day
on the seedling of barley grown sallow
in the past severe winter, moving against
the still cold wind, footsteps shown vivid.
Stepping on, treading on, yet, of course,
it's hardly reminiscent of the iron hooves
overriding, stamping down rising heads.
Rather, it's the treading on the sturdy
roots of our needy farming that are forced
to be plucked away more than ten times
in that dizzy world of crazy
trampling underfoot.
We keep stepping hard again and again
to make the roots ten times stronger
and to let them sprout up richly.
To have countless green stalks rise
standing above the harsh wintry darkness
under the free, blue sky, and to let the barley
raise our May, the month of bright green life,
we keep treading on the field.
It's our great pledge to the enduring farming
of us farmers dreaming of totally equal bread.
It's our paradoxical anger announcing
an endless fight with, and for, love
that we keep treading, gloriously treading.

A SILENT PRAYER FOR PEACE

I am meditating on Christ's mind
on the day He dispatched twelve disciples
to the world filled with darkness, the earth
where an evil spirit was flapping its feathers.

You are going to bring peace on earth;
you shouldn't take money bags with you.
You are a peace bringer;
you shouldn't take a food-bag either.
As a peace bringer,
you shouldn't have extra shoes.
Today I understand what you commanded;
that's the road to peace,
the right road to peace.

I am meditating on what Christ said
the day when He dispatched twelve disciples;
crop to harvest ripens with few, very few planters.

You are going to harvest peace;
you shouldn't stay at a house
of those who reject my peace.
You, peace planters, shouldn't sit
at a table that is ignorant of my peace.
Peace croppers, you, should beat dust off,
the dust you get on your shoes
from the ground that ignores my peace.
Today I understand what you meant;
that's the life of peace,
living peace.

Peace is our heart's desire;
peaceful reunification is our dream of dreams.
Do you hear the words of Christ
within everybody's shout all over the nation?

While your mouth wishes for peace,
your mind serves two masters.
If you truly wish peace,
you shouldn't keep dishes only for you;
if you truly want reunification,
you shouldn't hold a money bag only for you;
if you really desire peaceful reunification,
don't dream of a heavenly kingdom just for you.
Today I understand your words;
this is your call for peace,
your call for peace.

PEOPLE'S BREAD

Be equal, equal; be equal.
On this land the Lord provided, look,
a maidservant and her owner are living.
On the land the maid and the owner live
bread is not a sharing,
bread is not peace,
bread is not freedom,
it's not justice; no, no, it isn't.
It's none of these in the land the Lord provided
on the land the servant and her owner are living.

Be one, one; be one.
On this earth the Lord bled,
burglar nations and the people
of the plundered nations live together.
On the earth they are living
bread is not liberation,
bread is not history,
bread is not a race,
it's not reunification; no, no, it isn't.
It's none of these in the land He commanded oneness,
on the land the burglars and the robbed live together.

Oh listen, bread is the poor people's chains;
bread is a whip to lash people;
bread is a rope to tie the innocents;
ah, it's the weapon to kill the soul.

But, but—if that nation comes here,
bread would be equality;
bread would be peace;
it would be liberation. If

the heavenly kingdom should come down here,
bread would be love to share;
bread would be joy to have together;
it would be Holy Communion to make one;
bread, bread, bread would be
the heaven people propped up together.
Waiting for that day,
waiting for that nation
makes us thirsty,
thirsty,
thirsty.

WHEN YOU HOLD UP A BOWL OF NOODLES

A day's work is over
for a one-day worker.
You roll up dense steam
from a bowl of fresh noodles.

As the dinner-cooking smoke rises high
over a southern village at sunset,
you hold up a bowl of noodles to the sky.

Immense is
the silence of a dish of honest poverty;
immeasurable is
the generosity of pure simplicity.

With a cup of crude rice wine,
twilight brings you relaxation;
wide open in front of the gate
is the quiet moonlight.

PROVERB POEM IV

A thief is no remedy for poverty.
Who in this land? Who would stand up honestly?
There are inhabitants here, and that's all.
What else is there in the land ruined by monsters?
What is a living thing? Nothing.
Is there history?
Are there songs?
Is there the living? No.
Is there any movement? Love? Customs?
No, no. They are all dead.
The sea of a false rumor. A bored sky.
A plain where nothing moves, cars, and cornstalks.
Soil only to become dust.
Rotten village cottages, wooden floors.
Legends of love, all murdered.
The rain of death has never stopped.

A MINE

Don't lay a mine anymore.
Let's teach love on the road we walk,
under a thicket, and in their words.
Teaching how to play piano, my friend,
let's dig again and throw away
the kind of love we are fed up with;
saying so, let's get rid of things like that.

No more mines.
Let's teach love on our way,
under a thicket, and in their words.
Let's teach piano.
Absolutely not anymore
the kind of love we are tired of
and things like that.

MY BABY

Scared, my baby doesn't want to sleep.
Once fallen asleep, that's the end, he thinks,
and he would sleep forever, below ground.
My baby, why are you afraid of eternal sleep?
I don't understand it because that's what I want.
But not you; you should get up in the morning
when the early subway train passes by.
For my part, it goes opposite.
Buried in the ground, becoming soil or water,
I wish to fall asleep that way.
What do you think? I know Mom doesn't like it.
You are here in this winter; you are in this room.
My baby, don't be fearful; no fear;
have a sweet sleep, my baby.
When you sleep, you will be in Heaven.

HAVE YOU SEEN THIS WOMAN?

Chimney Woman was living in our town,
and she is missing. Suddenly one day,
she disappeared.
She might have risked a trip to Seoul.

By any chance have you seen a woman like this?
A woman around 50 years old:
she laughs, grinning, when she sees anybody;
she doesn't use an umbrella when it rains;
she may be wearing half-burnt clothes;
her face may show charcoal soot,
yet her hair may bear a chignon;
she may have white rubber shoes on.

To the normal eye
she looks like an insane woman,
but she seldom commits a sinful act.
The only thing she did wrong,
you might think, is that she had to steal
bread to eat and slept in the street.

We are looking for Chimney Woman.
If you happen to see her,
please give her this message:
people on Gold Crane Street
of Kongju City are looking for her;
don't face hard times in strange places
and come back to Gold Crane Street,
home for you.

Chimney Woman—the nickname of the missing woman in this poem.

CHUANGTZŬ POEM XXX

No matter whether I ride on the ninety-thousand-li clouds
of Sun Wukung or I lie down on a crowded street,
there is no way of escaping from an insect of agonies
awfully shivering its body inside a vein.
That's a lullaby coming from the organ.
That's the taste of cooked rocambole, a spring-time herb
freshly grown.
What's peculiar about agony?
Things familiar to the eye suddenly overlap and wriggle
or walk, coming head over heels;
that's what it is.

A SPRIG OF PLANTAIN LILY

The whistle I give
doesn't produce sound.

With the lips pursed round,
I draw blue breath out of the depth,
but it doesn't make a tune.

And yet I whistle when I am sad
to let the whole sad air get out of mind.

Cut into a word or two,
a scream may ring in the sound of wind.

A sprig of plantain lily
getting wet in the autumn rain
with its mouth closed:

That is
my whistle.

FROM A TREE TO A TREE

Because of the darkness inside a tree,
the tiny, faint light lit in it is trembling.
Because of the wind inside a tree,
a small tree planted in it is shaking.

I want to see you and listen to you
    in that tree.
I want to feel you with my whole body
    and figure out what you are.

I wish to call you loud,
dash to you, and hold your hands.

If now, here, all gathered,
the poor mind, cold mind, sorrowful mind
sharing your countless words on every leaf
could meet and rub against each other,

each of your branches would bear
the fruit of joy, I believe.

A LITTLE LOVE SONG

Look, my dear,
a flower lantern lightens.
It brightens the love between us
a hundred miles long and then
comes to the riverside in the evening.
You see the stars flowing like a river
to the dusky west.
Can we get a star and lighten our eyes
as the flower lantern does?
Shall we advance with brightened eyes
till the night falls and we become the last dark?
When the wind and grass all lie on the ground,
who would turn the lantern light off, Darling?
No need to put the light off
if we, becoming the dark
or becoming the star floating on water,
have to go to the dusky west,
following a flower lantern that lightens
hundred of miles and our eyes.

LYING IN A HALL

In this world, I've been miserable
without even a room just for me, but I'm going
to lie down in the hall of a palatial mansion
and take a nap with ramie clothes on;
relaxed, I'll enjoy the cuckoo's song.

In the other world to come sooner or later,
I'll have flower-marble-floor washed clean
where bamboo shoots will be set fresh.
Why don't you visit me feeling carefree
when the sun sets between strawberry leaves?

Our life has been affectionate and beautiful in a way
as we, with arms around each other's shoulders, got wet
in a shower in the field, or carrying a fodder bag
on our backs coming home in the evenings.
All this can't be finished on a rainbow in this world.

When we climbed a snowy mountain,
the worn-out shoes didn't matter much.
The stream from a compost pile would comfort us
when there was trouble in a garlic field.

All these things are the bases leading
to the wooden floor of a huge mansion in that world.
When we meet again at the end of daily routine,
let's not pull out the hands of sorrow,
but let's meet again with our flowery minds.
The spring in that world would be ours anyway.

I HAVE TO RETURN

Having gone to the one I had missed much,
I have to return without seeing.
Avoiding the eyes watching me in hiding, secluded,
and passing the dark bottom of a bridge
and a broad expanse of fields,
across hills, one after another,
I, with a ripe bellflower's mind, go to see her,
close enough, yet I have to turn back.

Once called,
she would rush to me
as if winged, but I turn my eyes,
hard though it is to keep them off,
and come back without calling.
Lest her burning wish and hope for my coming
should break,
I have to return to my place without contact.

THE DREAM OF A CROSS XII

We were not fearful at all, despite the fact that the streets were struck by a bunch of stray bullets, and traps were laid here and there so that our weakness couldn't cross over. We did not scatter at all. No matter who—the boys with dirty hands polishing passerbys' shoes in front of the post office, a butcher with bloody hands wringing a fowl's neck in Yongdong Market, or a student with white hands turning pages—all got together and formed one big stream of resistance. With burning eyes, we, the weak, watched all night those cold and stubborn faces being carried along with stray bullets, army codes, and verbal orders or falling into each other's arms. Many times, covered with ironclad protectors, they tried hard to force us to collapse. We, however, did not scatter at all. No matter who—a young woman pouring wine in Hwanggŭm-dong, a hungry shoeshine boy holding an empty gun, or a mother standing by her son's bloody head—we were all one, just one unity. We were determined not to scatter, not at all, until the nails driven into our hearts finally get pulled out. Meanwhile, a blue heaven was held in our hearts.

MINEFIELDS AND MIGRANTS

The day when the hard coals
made in North Korea were unloaded
at Inchon Port, crossing over
the half-century-old wall,
the small port was totally filled
with everybody's curiosity.
The pollacks caught in the sea near Ch'ongjin
have been popular at tables
in South Korean restaurants.
Now at last, with minefields cleared away,
the south and north become one,
wishfully imagined, while
the sky was so cleanly blue.
Oh no, this morning, the news highlighted
the face of my younger friend who was arrested
for reading a North Korean book.
A flock of migratory birds have flown
back to the north, which is warm again.

A SMALL PUDDLE

Slowly, I walk down through
a small puddle in my mind
still tried, exhausted.

Slowly, slowly,
I step downward.

Once reached, the bottom,
another world would be,
momentarily, suddenly,
open in my mind; so I believe.

Not to say
I would like to believe,
but I already do believe it.

A small puddle:
that's my black hole.

JUDGMENT

Now I give up hope for the rich.
In front of their feet, now I throw away hope
    for those who don't share.
Hope for the learned people, I give up.
Also hope for those whose houses got smaller,
    now I give up.

Now I give up absolutely everything in the world;
resentment and curse are no exception.

I know what I can do now: I must live poorly.
I neither cry, saying, "son of a bitch,"
nor look at the flame and cry.

I know what I can do now is to dream of
the great dream that is exposed to the bellows
    in my poverty.
You or me and nobody else! We know
this world is waiting for judgment by fire.

A PASSERBY

When I pass by here, a thick fog sets in.
The wind blows toward me,
clouds come up, the lightning flashes
when I pass by.
Sorrow comes down like rain—
my gosh—when I pass by.

No rain, no rain now, please.
I'm the one who travels now.

Where I pass, there lies solitude;
where I pass, there comes regret;
oh my god, only anger hangs over.
With anger and obstinacy overwhelming,
liquor falls down like rain
on my passing way.

No rain, no rain, please.
If I get wet, it makes a tragedy, right?

When I pass by,
there lie only promise and credit.

THE DREAM OF AN INFERIOR

In the long factory night,
fatigue attacks
over my cold shoulders.

At the humming of a sewing machine,
I dream of getting on the dream-like machine
with two-timers working all night.
With the frozen hands of an inferior,
I cut a rosy dream,
snip a vain dream,
and put bloody leather patterns
up on the stand one after another.

An inferior as yet,
I want to get on the machine;
riding on it
with a general's dignified face,
I want to make warm clothes
that would shield frozen bodies;
I want to sew a torn livelihood.

The whole body shivering,
an inferior as yet,
I am scissoring, hammering.
With a dream of connecting
all the divided things into one
riding on the sewing machine,
a little, low worker
is running pliantly
on the complex streets.
Look, the dawn stars twinkle
over the worn-out forehead!

MOTHER

Mother,
I grew up sucking your milk
out of the thin breast when you were weeding
under the blazing sun in the southern hungry summer;
at times you nourished me with some tender and good food
that all should have gone to your body.
I grew up like a spider, eating off my own mother's flesh.

Even though I grew poorly on poor porridge,
and though I struggle as a laborer with little education,
I've never stolen anything.
Neither have I eaten the bread of idleness
nor given other people troubles.
The only person whom I made sad in my life
is you, Mother.

You only wished a peaceful, happy
family life even in poverty.
I've worked hard, justly demanded,
and conscientiously fought for our new life.
The more we fought, the tougher hardships we faced.
You get more anxious, give up things in despair,
and implore me to stop standing up.
Mother, in your sixties, you still work as a visiting maid;
you have a wish, and that is the very dream of us all.
Because we were poor, we couldn't study, and because
we've been suffering humiliation, disdainful treatment,
        and hard labor,
our wish for a peaceful and happy family
is the earnest, reasonable wish of all of us.

Oh, Mother!

In yourself, our enemy stays.
He is cruel enough to override our wish for a happy family
and to sit cross-legged in your heart wilily as a viper
of submission, egoism, greed, and idleness.
With their most stubborn and toughest tongue,
the wicked enemy cuts into our humaneness,
which is our weakness, for a dirty trick.

I know I drive a nail into your heart;
you are the only person in the world I do this to.
For your sincere wish,
all the mothers' earnest wish,
for the recapture of happiness,
we, becoming ungrateful to our parents,
go to that brutal battlefield
crying and crying,
leaving our mothers behind.

We will win and come back
with glorious face and will make
a ceremonial, big bow to you.
Till then, we will be the worst unfilial
children who truly love their mothers.
Shedding bitter tears,
we leave for the battlefield.
So long, Mother,
Mother.

IN A CLOSET

In the back room where I sleep, there are
many kinds of seeds scattered in disorder:
the seeds of rice, potatoes, perilla, pepper,
red bean, soy bean, green pea, and so on.
Some of them are in a straw bag, others in a jar,
some in a bottle gourd hanging on the wall.
When I lie down with eyes closed,
I can hear them breathing.
Their talking voice spreads all over,
and the colors of their creams glimmer.
I love the honest whisper of these seeds
and their dream's colors so much that I
sleep with them, and we dream together.
That's why I am waiting
for the pleasure of another meeting.

LABOR RICE

I want to eat rice in which blood circulates;
I want to eat rice, living and lively:
rice eaten to be used for a clean life,
eaten to become clean strength.
The strength used as needed becomes rice,
living rice—of and for labor.

I don't want to eat rice moving ahead of life;
neither do I want to eat rice, not living and lively.
You should give lifeless rice to the lifeless.
If you can't see rice clearly,
you can't see life clearly, either.

I want to eat living rice.
If life is clear, rice is clear, too;
if rice is clear, so is life.
I want to eat blood-circulating rice,
living rice—of and for labor.

THE SOUND OF THE EMILLE BELL

Ever since I started working at a blast furnace,
I've been hearing the sound of the Emille Bell.
Facing metal-stain spots, legs trembling,
and the lung turning to junk because of poison gas,
we make iron to be carried away somewhere;
it becomes the sound of the Emille Bell
anywhere the iron goes, and the sound comes back to us.

The iron is carried away
and gets stained with many friends' blood.
It cuts their flesh, is carried somewhere,
and deceives us.
Made into a rotary press, it sneers at 4,000 Won
daily wages; made into a radio, it mocks
at a weekly 80-hour program, and made
into a TV set, it laughs at year-round work.

The iron made out of burned muscles, carried away,
turns to their family cars, not ours, and their trophies,
high buildings, airplanes, and weapons;
then it produces the sound of the Emille Bell
and comes back to us.

There tolls the Emille Bell
out of the ironware we meet, leaving factory gates.
There rings the bell out of ironware
which mixed our poverty and muscles;
the howling Emille Bell rings out.

Emille—(pronounced "eh-mi-lee") a nickname for the fuge bell originally placed at Pongdŏksa, a Buddhist temple, now preserved in Kyŏngju Museum.

WHEN GRASS-INSECTS CHIRP

As I turn forty, yearning for sounds like
the chirping of grass-insects over there,
I call the names of those I miss, calls being
muffled among the tiny withered grasses.
At a time when survival means nothing but
panting, while no longer are dear ones around,
either having left far away or gone into hiding.
Just being unable to depart, some are behind
wandering about in the dark, with only their
groaning echoes, mixed in my calls.
At the very end of their moan, also you,
the sick person, try hard to cry out,
the cry mingled with my calls.

FLYING BIRDS

When I look at where you are,
my friends,
after I dreamed of a flying bird,
so many birds fly there.
I see birds flying dazzlingly
like a great outcry once and for all
as you cut the chains
and cross over the spears.

ON A SNOWY NIGHT

You who are being pursued
with no place to stop,
it's snowing tonight, isn't it?
I will wait for you until dawn
with the lights on.
Come running all night!
Before the snow stops, let's
watch it with our swollen eyes;
let's watch the grass roots
forsaken throughout the winter
now fallen asleep at last
blanketed with snow.

SHORT GRASSES TOGETHER

Though the wind is new every day,
short grasses should live leaning
against each other by themselves.
Let's not try to win over the world.
We can't be flowers,
nor can we be trees.
Totally open even to the end
of the passing wind,
our backs feel warm:
simply with a lonely drop of water
on an unbearably lonely day,
with a hungry drop of water alone
on an extremely hungry day,
and just with the light of streetlamps
when it gets dark.

By looking at their neighbor's wet eyes,
short grasses among themselves
alleviate sorrow, leaning on each other.

TO JONAH

She goes to the sea in secret.
Toward the waves of darkness
expanding without end—
neither land nor the sky,
neither this world nor the other one,
she goes out to the sea.
Unable to control the blast of the wind
approaching her heart heatedly,
she chooses the sea
although she knows the sin
which she can neither avoid nor hide.

For wind and waves are still calm,
the starry sky is boundless yet,
and the unknown island is still desolate,
she chooses the sea, while hearing
the choking, warning sound of waves
saying, "Come back, come back."
In the middle of the Lord's silence,
she can't recede,
nor can she advance;
she becomes a missing child
drifting about on the deep blue sea
as a circle, a circle;
she becomes the one who runs away
to Tarshish.

BLESSING

Man is not blessed with wings.
He is allowed only to have
a head with eyes to look up at the stars,
two legs to cross over a hill step by step,
a warm hand to hold his neighbor—
all that can be awarded
for hard work under the sun.

AN ISLAND

When you were waves, I was a slope, so to say.
When you wished to be warm wind towards land,
I was a cliff standing upright far away.
One day you came close as a silent current,
touching secretly a quiet rock, and then—so said—
just returned with forgiveness left behind.
You lived, so it's said, only looking at the rough slope back.
Only at the moment a chest trouble appeared on your skin,
I noticed your deepening ailment.
When the uncontrollable waves surged from your heart one day,
striking my back, and the tide retreated, tumbling down,
I, shocked, looked back only to find you
drowned, floating, on a way never to return.
One raging surf was enough to knock me down;
trying hard to catch you to the end
where I lay flat as dead mud flat.
Winter came again to this dismal sea, still waving,
and time was for long confining me
stuck there, motionless.

WHO ARE YOU?

You told me to come to the river, and I did.
At first, you had called on thousands of brilliant sunbeams,
then collected them all into the mountain shades, and then
told me to follow you to the desolate end of the river.
    Who are you?

When told to come to a wood, I went there to see you.
You sent the waving shadow of a tree to the meeting place
making me stay up all the days and nights with red leaves.
    Where are you?

Told to cross over a ridge, I did so.
You sent a flock of wild geese to the pass, having
one of them travel far beyond the skyline while
turning its head back at me over again.
    What is your intent?

You called me out from the trail to the world,
and then, in the flooding crowds on the earthly streets,
you have been on and off again and again.
    Who are you?

You brought me pain and wounds first.
In front of a dish of salt to clean the wound
on an empty tideland, you wrote no pain
with no meaning on earth; you were silent.

Who are you?
I am a feeble candlelight even shaking at an insect's cry.
I let my whole body burn in the fire you made,
but you spent your days with darkness
eighteen thousand times as much my little soul.
    Who are you?

RAIN ON A LONG DAY

It's raining outside the jail window.
As I look at the cloudy sky,
the raindrops make rings in my mind.
Even the visible part of the sky
is broken into pieces.
My heart broken, I can't cry out;
for the one I miss, I can't run.
Nor can I be sad.
Among inmates, each tattooed with sorrow
on his face and heart, I can't afford to live
soothing my pain all alone.
I only chew sadness as I chew barley.
I only wipe hatred as I clean up each dish.
With a black hood on,
I can't be free as a sparrow under a tree;
nor can I walk around as does a mouse
over the iron gate.
They claim my offense against what to follow,
but I was more concerned with neglecting
what I believed to be right;
I was afraid of the guilt of doing nothing right.
That's all, and now I am confined away from
both stormy clouds over the northern bars
and rain streaks beyond the south.
I am thinking of what is blocked over the north
and what is snatched away on the southern side.
On a long day, the longer it rains,
the more I long for the dear one, flying
my wet mind over the fence and mountains.

DHARMA POEM V

Step down to a valley;
the naked body of water, inside,
is clearly seen through between rocks.
I put my feet in the water, and the sand
at the bottom feels like water's bones.
White and clean sands that have washed off
the filth of time completely.
The lapping current flows into my blood vessels.
The transparent blood color in the water color.
A-ha!
Only now I seem to know well
this is what I have flown up to now,
I have come up to here, and that
this is it: the place I wanted.
A valley ...
Dug deep here is a singular mind.
A deep hollow, deep water.

DHARMA POEM XVI

The sun is stark-naked.
It stripped itself of its skin and threw it away.
Pieces of its flesh were falling down;
a Siberian alder catches them to try on
while the sunrays glaring and swaying.
Having watched all this for some time,
I came to wish to take all my clothes off,
to be completely naked.
Sitting on the waterside, I watched the sunbeams
falling into the water, sinking into its bottom.
Oh well, then! Whatever happens!
Undressed at once, I plopped into the water
and splashed there along with the sunrays.

DHARMA POEM XVII

I push my body into it.
Squeezing myself in
between the hurdled rocks,
forcing me to cramp into this chink,
I wish to pour the sound of water
that swings slowly within me;
I wish to stagnate there.
Wish to be filled full in the gap
between the rocks;
wish to lick its mind where it reflects
the color of the blue-moss-grown age
with my rolling, innocent waves.
The voice of his call and my call
being folded small in the water's echo,
one life to live is passing silently
as the shadow of water.
I hear the sound of water flowing
transparently within me, while sitting
inside the rock for a short while.

LOOKING AT A TRADITIONAL DRESSER

A grandfather of the Poch'ŏn'gyo Regiment
at the end of the Tonghak Incident
was the wind going through
pine groves and bamboo groves;
a grandmother was only watching
the starlight and the moonlight.

Carried by clouds, an uncle went to North Kando, Manchuria,
and another uncle, a worker drafted by the Japanese,
came back in the form of ash. With all this,
a grandmother was just washing clothes.
Her love being pure white,
she was only washing clothes
as if trying to bleach cotton yarn.

When her blue-tile house was burning,
the smoke reminded her of the shaman practice
    of burning sacrificial paper.
She kept watching only the sky and land nearby
and combing her pretty hair as the sun set over the far hills;
eventually, she became an ornamental design
    made of paulownia;
she became a design on this dresser.

Poch'ŏn'gyo—one of the religious organizations of ancient times.
Tonghak Incident—a Korean civil war in 1894 between the government forces and the Tonghak Army, largely consisting of farmers, led by Chŏn Pong-jun. The Incident eventually led to the Ch'ing (China)-Japan War, 1894-96.

A FARMHAND'S SONG

Let me shake the river and wake it up.
Let me clear up the harmful dark
in the servants' quarters and open
the heavenly crossbar in our village
hagridden and fallen asleep.
With the storm, animal's roaring,
and cold rice meal, all being overcome,
strength joyfully gushes out
once I step on earth.
As the smell of grass in this beloved land
makes my bosom heave in ecstasies,
I would have a sweet dream
even in the night of nightmare; then I
like to sweep yards from sunup to sundown.
Let me sweep this country's yards
so clean that you can pick up and eat
even a grain of spilt rice.

CHAGALL'S SEOUL V

Under the naked roadside trees,
a soldier of the republic is violating a woman.
Resting on the streetlights, the Seoul poets
are whistling gloomily, gloomily
at the sight of flapping skirts.
Revolution is repeated while women
bake bread, their waist hurting; love is only
rough and licentious, a bucktooth projecting.
In darkness, the citizens get older,
and hope has snatched many things.
Ah, I wish to be a farmer in a warm land
taking care of a dreaming goat
that holds a barberry shrub.

A NAME

The further the night advances,
the more seriously we need to call somebody.
If we don't call that name,
if we forget the name even for a second,
we hear a heated voice that calls us,
a voice with a whip.

The darker the night falls,
the more we need to go to somebody.
When we stop going
or give up going,
we hear the sound of painful footsteps
walking to us over the sword traces.

We have to call someone;
we have to go to someone
even if it's our brothers' cold hands
that press down on our windpipe
in the broad daylight.

Even if, someday, our blood may turn
to a sickle to be used, warmed,
in the rice field of our home,
today we must go to him
with the pressed neck being pulled out.
We must call his name today
in order to become a rock for him
as we fall down while calling him;
in order for us to be a totem pole for him
as we stop, standing upright, we must.

ON HISTORY

Those who fought at that time
didn't leave the truth behind;
they didn't even have time to do.
They simply laid their bones
on certain burning ridges somewhere.

After decades
there echoes the shouting of the dead bodies
exposed under the dark earth
in the excavation site which leads to Piagol.
And there lies solitude like black ink
over the old mountains, now rising high.

A SONG

I stand on this riverside
to convey a phrase: I love you.
The gust here and the storm there
prevent me from crossing the river.

Sometimes, I stand on this hill
to return a phrase: forget, forget about it.
Roaring thunder here and high cliff there in the storm
prevent me from approaching, moving to you.

I am stuck like a flower open on a faraway cliff
and like a silverfish with ephemeral life going against
the rough river between suffocating rocks.

BEFORE A GOLDEN SPIDER

I am off today, Mother.
Actually, I haven't slept for a long time;
I have neither eaten nor cried so long.
Mother, it has been long since we got caught
in a web woven by a golden spider.
It's really scary, Mother.
The golden spider is approaching us.
Mother, we are scared.
The golden spider will eat us
and then will pull out white threads.

THE WEST SEA

Because you might be staying there,
I haven't been to the West Sea yet.

That sea must not be unusual, I imagine;
little crabs get in and out of holes in the black silt,
and the sea always tosses and tumbles
far beyond a broad expanse of field.

I think I'll save the place I haven't visited
just for your own sojourn;
there won't be room for you if I visit everywhere.

Another sea I haven't been to
always surges only in my heart.

A RIVER

People say I am lonesome.
That's because I followed a grove of poplar
at nightfall one day.

They say I am sick.
That's because my face has turned black
in smoky pollution.

But I've never been lonesome or sick.
I've just passed through
their town in a hurry.

Not stopping what comes to me,
not stopping what leaves me,
I am the tears that flow in their eyes.

A STAR

Early in the morning,
feeling like passing water outside,
I came out to the yard.
The dog lying on the ground
wags its tail.
Some little water is in the dog bowl;
there may have passed a spell of rain.
On the water staying in the bowl,
a star casts limpid light.
Up there in the sky,
I see a star that woke up early as I did
looking down at the empty dog bowl.

TWIN CHESTNUTS

I picked up one of the fresh chestnuts
collected in a wicker basket
and found beautiful twins sitting
side by side inside the same shell.
Interested, I put them on the palm
of my hand and examined
their appearance carefully.
One isn't larger or smaller than the other;
one doesn't slight or disparage the other.
The same tree has borne fruit
in spite of violent wind and rain;
the twins settled in a friendly posture
inside the same shell.
They make me imagine:
our country reunified would look
exactly like this.

MY EYES FOR YOU

a will by a man who left his native land

Being able to give my eyes to you, I am delighted.
I thank God for helping me have this perfect pleasure
and am grateful to my neighbors as well.
Till today, since my parents gave me my life,
I've been living just for one purpose
and now leave the world at the heavenly calling.
People pity me for having a fatal cancer,
but I know a joyful time has come to me.
Unbelievably calm and even courtly,
I am glad I can donate my eyes to you.
After my death, they will still be alive in your body
that has been lost in the dark for a long time.
They will emit honorable light;
they will lead a long, long life beyond death.
When you finally have to leave the world,
you may like to give the precious eyes
and something equally important to those
who are in acute need, suffering.
This is the love of giving and receiving a body.
I've just started appreciating the death of a family
that jumped into a deep marsh trying to save
their son who was drowning.

I hope a strong, unbreakable rope of love
can be led to the heart of our nation.
I am absolutely so happy right now.
The only wish I have before death
is that the little eyes that tie you and me
would become the origin of light for this country.

VISITING THE FAMILY GRAVE

The Full Moon Harvest Day,
a grave-visit day, is over, yet
the father is here, silent, before a grave;
on the dry grass, he put apples and pears
and a cup of *soju* drink instead of tears.
Far down there, a bunch of cosmos—
least mindful of him—is flowering.
Empty is the blue sky up there,
whatever that means.
Son, you left before your father.
Pulling the dry leaves of grass,
reminiscent of your sallow hair,
the father is crying deep in his mind.
Mountains with sad souls buried are also crying.
Son, you paid for the road to death with your body.
listen, Kŭmnamno hasn't changed since you left,
nor has the area near your school gate.
But the sorrowful people have been silent since then;
looking at each other, they have been silent;
so have the father and Mt. Mudŭng
without you around.

Kŭmnamno—street in Kwangju, a city in South Cholla.

CERTAIN TIES

The bullet that missed my neck by chance sometime ago
may have gone through someone's body;
another one which mysteriously disappeared
was suddenly running today
toward the back of my head—
that was unavoidable.

That is something which I mustn't avoid,
something which will grow bigger if I do
and will come back faster than before.

The bullets driven in our cowardice
and in the burning sunset over Kŭmnamno.

The bullets coming blindly toward our head again
after passing the Kwangju River,
passing the bloody desert in Afghanistan
and piles of the torn bodies of the freedom fighters,
then crossing the Han River in Seoul.

I have decided that I won't avoid
those unavoidable ties again.
Rather, I've decided that I'll stop the chain
of the vicious ties from linking further
by devoting my life.

About the Poets

Chang Chŏng-il (1962)

Born in Kyungsand Pukdo. Published poems since 1984. His books of poetry include *Catching a Taxi in the Middle of the Street* (1988).

Chang Yŏng-su (1947)

Born in Kangwondo, graduated from Seoul University with a major in French. Published poems since 1973. His books of poetry include *Like Butterfly, Nay, Like Light* (1987).

Ch'oe Sŭng-ho (1954)

Born in Kangwondo. Published poems since 1977. His four books of poetry include *The Joy of a Worldly City* (1990).

Ch'oe Tong-ho (1948)

Born in Kyonggido. Professor of Korean literature at Koryo University. His numerous publications include *Where Is the Woodpecker Hiding?* (1995) and other volumes of poetry.

Ch'oe Tu-sŏk (1955)

Born in Seoul, graduated from Seoul University with a major in Korean literature for teachers. Published poems since 1980. His books of poetry include *The Sky Blanket* (1990).

Chŏng Hŭi-Sŏng (1945)

Born in Kyongsang Namdo, graduated from Seoul University with a major in Korean literature. Published poems since 1970. His books of poetry include *From One Longing to Another* (1991).

Ha Chong-o (1954)

Born in Kyongsang Pukdo. Published poems since 1975. Many volumes of his poetry include *Flowers Bloom Just for Us* (1988).

Hwang Chi-u (1952)

Born in Cholla Namdo, graduated from Seoul University with a major in aesthetics. Published poems since 1980. His many books of poetry include *Lotus Flowers in a Crab's Eye* (1990).

Kang Ŭn-kyo (1945)

Born in Hamgyong Namdo, graduated from Yonsei University with a major in English. She teaches at Pusan University. Published poems since 1968. Numerous volumes of her poetry include *Letters Inside the Wall* (1992).

Ki Hyŏng-do (1960-89)

Born in Kyonggido, graduated from Yonsei University with a major in politics. Published poems since 1985. He committed suicide while working as a reporter. His posthumous book of poetry is *Black Leaves in the Mouth* (1989).

Kim Chŏng-hwan (1954)

Born in Seoul, graduated from Seoul University with a major in English. Published poems since 1980. Numerous volumes of his poetry include *An Age of Hope* (1992).

Kim Chun-t'ae (1948)

Born in Cholla Namdo, graduated from Choson University with a major in German. Published poems since 1969, including "Ah Kwangju, Our Nation's Cross," which caused his dismissal from teaching at a high school. Six books of his poetry include *Sword and Earth* (1989).

Kim Hye-sun (1955)

Born in Kyongsang Pukdo, graduated from Kon'guk University with a major in Korean literature. Published poems since 1979. Her four books of poetry, all quite modernistic, include *Our Negatives* (1990).

Kim Myŏng-su (1945)

Born in Kyongsang Pukdo. Published poems since 1977. His four volumes of poetry include *A Zone of Needle-Leaf Trees* (1991).

Kim Nam-ju (1946)

Born in Cholla Namdo, studied English literature at Chonnam University. Published poems since 1974. Numerous volumes of his poetry include *In This Good World (1992)* and *Selected Poems Written in Jail* (1992).

Kim Sa-in (1955)

Born in Chungchong Pukdo, graduated from Seoul University with a major in Korean literature. Published poems since 1981. His books of poetry include *Letters I Write at Night* (1987).

Kim Yong-t'aek (1948)

Born in Cholla Pukdo. An activist, started publishing poems in 1982. Five volumes of his poetry include *Flower Letters of Yearning* (1989).

Ko Chae-jong (1957)

Born in Cholla Namdo. Published poems since 1984. His books of poetry include *Love Stopping in the Windy Pine Tree Woods* (1987) and *Human Light* (1992).

Ko Chŏng-hŭi (1948-91)

Born in Cholla Namdo, graduated from Han'guk Seminary. An activist woman poet, started publishing poems in 1975. Numerous volumes of her poetry include *A Beautiful Person* (1991) and *All the Disappearing Things Leave a Space Behind* (1992).

Ko Hyŏng-nyŏl (1954)

Born in Cholla Namdo, published poems since 1979. His five books of poetry include *A Little Boy* (1990). He co-authored a three-poet anthology, *Embrace* (1993).

Na T'ae-jun (1945)

Born in Chungchong Namdo, he is a school teacher. Published poems since 1971. Six books of his poetry include *One Scale of Life* (1986).

Pak Che-ch'ŏn (1945)

His name is also spelled Park Je-chun and Park Chech-on in two selections of his poems in English translation. Born in Seoul, studied Korean literature at Tong-guk University, participated in the University of Iowa's International Writing Program. Winner of several literary prizes, his publications include thirteen volumes of poetry, the most recent one being *Tree Sarira* (1995).

Pak Chŏng-man (1946-88)

Born in Cholla Pukdo, graduated from Kyonghui University with a major in Korean literature, started publishing poems in 1968. His eight books of poetry include the posthumous *Selected Poems of Pak Chŏng-man* (1990).

Pak Mong-gu (1956)

Born in Cholla Namdo, graduated from Chonnam University with a major in English. Started publishing poems in 1977. His six books of poetry include *Coming Out of a Theatre One Day* (1992).

Pak Nam-chŏl (1953)

Born in Kyongsang Pukdo, graduated from Kyonghui University with a major in Korean literature, started publishing poems in 1979. His books of poetry include *Perverse Talks at a Russian House* (1991).

Pak No-hae (1957)

Born in Cholla Namdo, an activist labor worker, has published poems since 1983. His first book of poetry was *Labor Dawn* (1984), followed by selected poems, *Tying a Hairband* (1991).

Pak Un-sik (1946)

Born in Chungchong Pukdo. His books of poetry include *All Joyful, Drinking and Eating* (1989).

Paek Mu-san (1955)

Born in Kyongsang Pukdo, started publishing poems in 1984. His books of poetry include *Standing in the Dawn at Mipo Bay* (1990).

Song Ki-wŏn (1947)

Born in Cholla Namdo, graduated from Chung-ang University with a major in creative writing. Started publishing poems and short stories in 1974. His books of poetry include *Red Flowers in the Mind* (1990).

Song Yŏng-hŭi (1945)

Born in Kyonggido, graduated from Kyonggi University with a major in Korean literature. Her first book of poetry was *To You, Jonah* (1994).

To Chong-hwan (1954)

Born in Chungchong Pukdo, graduated from Chungbuk University with a major in Korean literature for teachers. An activist, started publishing poems in 1984. His books of poetry include *Even Though I Leave You Now* (1989).

Yi Na-myŏng (1945)

Born in Kangwondo, started publishing poems in 1994. Her second book of poetry is *Green Is the Center* (1996).

Yi Sang-guk (1946)

Born in Kangwondo, published poems since 1976. His books of poetry include *We Are Going to a Town* (1992).

Yi Si-yŏng (1949)

Born in Cholla Namdo, graduated from Sorabol Fine Arts College with a major in creative writing. Started publishing poems in 1969. Numerous books of his poetry include *An Interval* (1996).

Yi Sŏng-bok (1952)

Born in Kyongsang Pukdo, graduated from Seoul University with a major in French. Published poems since 1977. His books of poetry include *The End of That Summer* (1990).

Yi Tong-sun (1950)

Born in Kyongsang Pukdo, graduated from Kyongbuk University with a major in Korean literature. Started publishing poems in 1973. Several books of his poetry include *Those Fools Are Becoming More Foolish* (1992).

Yi Yŏng-jin (1956)

Born in Cholla Namdo, a graduate of Usok University with a major in Korean literature. Started publishing poems in 1976. His first book of poetry was *Korean War and Melon Seeds* (1986).

Note: The original selection of poets for this anthology included **Ch'oe Sŭng-ja**, **Ryu Si-hwa**, and **Yi Chŏng-u**. Regrettably, because of problems in obtaining their copyright permission, they are not included here.

About the Translator / Editor

Ko Won is the pen name of Ko Sung-Won; his Christian name is Andrew Ko. Born in Korea, graduated from Tong-guk University, studied English literature at Queen Mary College, University of London, came to the United States in early 1964, earned his M.F.A. in English (creative writing) from the University of Iowa, and a Ph.D. in comparative literature from New York University. He taught at Brooklyn College of CUNY and the University of California, Riverside; he is currently teaching at the University of La Verne, California. A bilingual poet, winner of the Kansas City Star Award for poetry (1966) and many other prizes, his publications include 12 volumes of poetry written in Korean, two volumes of poetry in English—*The Turn of Zero* (1974) and *Some Other Time* (1990)—two books of translations from Korean into English—*Contemporary Korean Poetry* (1970) and *South Korean Poets of Resistance* (1980)—and a scholarly work, *Buddhist Elements in Dada: A Comparison of Tristan Tzara, Takahashi Shinkichi, and Their Fellow Poets* (1977). A member of P.E.N. Center USA West, publisher/editor of *The Literary Realm/Munhak segye*, he also directs the Kŭlmaru Institute of Literature, Los Angeles.